KU-214-578

# A Short-cut to Marketing the Library

## CHANDOS
### INFORMATION PROFESSIONAL SERIES

Series Editor: Ruth Rikowski
(email: Rikowskigr@aol.com)

Chandos' new series of books are aimed at the busy information professional. They have been specially commissioned to provide the reader with an authoritative view of current thinking. They are designed to provide easy-to-read and (most importantly) practical coverage of topics that are of interest to librarians and other information professionals. If you would like a full listing of current and forthcoming titles, please visit our web site www.chandospublishing.com or email info@chandospublishing.com or telephone +44 (0) 1223 891358.

**New authors:** we are always pleased to receive ideas for new titles; if you would like to write a book for Chandos, please contact Dr Glyn Jones on email gjones@chandospublishing.com or telephone number +44 (0) 1993 848726.

**Bulk orders:** some organisations buy a number of copies of our books. If you are interested in doing this, we would be pleased to discuss a discount. Please email info@chandospublishing.com or telephone +44 (0) 1223 891358.

# A Short-cut to Marketing the Library

### Zuzana Helinsky

Chandos Publishing
Oxford · Cambridge · New Delhi

Chandos Publishing
TBAC Business Centre
Avenue 4
Station Lane
Witney
Oxford OX28 4BN
UK
Tel: +44 (0) 1993 848726
Email: info@chandospublishing.com
www.chandospublishing.com

Chandos Publishing is an imprint of Woodhead Publishing Limited

Woodhead Publishing Limited
Abington Hall
Granta Park
Great Abington
Cambridge CB21 6AH
UK
www.woodheadpublishing.com

First published in 2008

ISBN:
978 1 84334 425 4

British Library Cataloguing-in-Publication Data.
A catalogue record for this book is available from the British Library.

Typeset by Domex e-Data Pvt. Ltd.
Printed in the UK and USA.

Printed in the UK by 4edge Limited - www.4edge.co.uk

# Contents

# About the author

**Zuzana Helinsky** is a consultant specialising in services to the publishing and library community. She is a qualified librarian with wide international business experience. For the last 20 years she has worked in providing services to libraries around the world. Zuzana speaks regularly at international conferences and lectures for seminars and business classes.

Arriving in Sweden from the Czech Republic in 1969, she gained a degree in philology and history at Lund University and a master's in library and information science from Boras Bibliotekshogskola. She worked for several years in the serials department at Lund University before joining BTJ, Sweden's largest library service company, initially to upgrade its cataloguing system.

In the mid-1980s Zuzana created and managed BTJ's subscription service, which grew to US$25 million by the mid-1990s, when BTJ acquired another Swedish agent. She was then responsible for integration and rationalisation of the two businesses, offices and management. From the mid-1990s she was manager of international business for BTJ, creating new business worth $1.5 million in the Middle East, Turkey, Greece and Central Europe.

She was director of publisher relations for Prenax Global, an innovative international subscription management company. She set up and managed relationships with publishers all over the world, servicing offices in Sweden, the USA, Germany, France and England.

Zuzana's mother tongue is Czech and she is also fluent in Russian, Swedish and English. She has a working knowledge of Slavonic languages such as Slovak, Serbian and Polish, and Scandinavian languages such as Danish and Norwegian. She is a member of the executive of the Association of Subscription Agents and a member of the editorial board of *Serials* – the journal of the UK Serials Group.

# Acknowledgements

My special thanks go to Colin Harrison, former managing director of Everetts and a good friend and colleague. When this book was originally published in Sweden (in Swedish), it was Colin's idea that it might be beneficial to offer it to the wider English-speaking library world. To persuade me to do this he promised to help with the translation – although he probably often regretted this, as it was a difficult work to convert for a different readership. He was able to bring to the project his wide knowledge of libraries, librarians and library life not only in the UK but also in Australasia, North America and many other parts of the world. I greatly appreciated Colin's ideas about what to add and how to revise the 2006 Swedish edition in order to produce this English version.

In short, without Colin this book would not have existed.

# Introduction

> Not marketing your activities is like standing in a dark corner and winking at a girl. You know what you are doing but nobody else does. (Anon.)

I have been holding courses on marketing for libraries in several countries since 2001. The many delegates who have heard my approach to this topic have almost invariably agreed that the need for marketing is continually increasing. I have often been asked for some additional material to help participants to follow up after the course – and this small book is my contribution.

In most libraries there is, in the appropriate section, a great deal of literature on marketing. But when, as a library professional, you open one of these books, you will find it full of terms like profit, margins, revenue, marketing director, branding, maximising profit and so on – all apparently irrelevant to the library world. Marketing books, even those with a subtitle 'An introduction to…', are often 600 pages long.

Almost all the marketing examples in books aimed at the business sector are difficult for us librarians to relate to, because a library does not compete on price, but rather on knowledge, competence and relationships. So you probably feel that such books contain nothing relevant to you. These marketing books are of course aimed at a completely different audience, and one which has completely different assumptions from ours. They have no appreciation at all of what it is like to work in a library, or to try to market library services when you have almost no budget allocation for marketing and certainly no time to spend on it.

This intuitive reaction is both right and wrong. It is wrong because marketing is something which libraries should be working on, but in a rather different way from the more commercial approaches. It is at the same time right, because it is not at all easy to adapt such general-purpose books and models to our library environment. I hope for this reason that this little book about marketing will help. It is very simple in concept because it is determined not to frighten library professionals. If later you want go on and get a much deeper perspective, then there are many good books on the wider subject of marketing.

This book has as its starting point both traditional marketing and traditional library activities. It should be seen as a simple one-hour handbook which begins with an understanding of what life is really like in a library. It should serve as an inspiration and as food for thought, with the help of examples which illustrate my approach. I also want to provide some concrete suggestions and ideas for marketing in a library, and some thoughts about us as a professional group. This handbook absolutely does not set out to be an academic work with deep analysis, complicated theoretical models and difficult language; I am describing instead the models I have used in real library life, and which have worked successfully in many institutions.

Most people now recognise that we must market ourselves and our libraries, and there are many great libraries making wonderful marketing efforts. But there are still too many people in this industry who think that marketing is just not as important as most other activities in the library. I aim this book at all levels and all shades of opinion – at the experienced marketers as confirmation that their effort is not only justified but essential, and also at those who think that marketing is something difficult and way beyond their experience, and who for that reason would prefer to sit about and do nothing. I also address those who say 'I have no time for marketing'. Nobody can afford to ignore this issue now, and I will try to show you how to get started, or more probably (because you are almost certainly part of the way along the road already) how you can easily apply a systematic approach to marketing and thus obtain a better overview. There is already a lot of very good marketing work done in the library world, but I am convinced that we need to do even more. Most of all we need to change how the library is perceived as a whole by people 'outside', and here we need more strenuous efforts. But I have also come to understand after many years how little importance people place on what I call 'owner marketing'. This means getting our message over properly to the decision-makers in our world – not so much the library director, or whatever the title, but those who control our budget and therefore our destiny: the university chancellor, the local councillors or the board directors.

Owner marketing is very often almost forgotten. Of course each library is unique, and every library employee is unique, *but*:

- all of us can do more marketing (except in the case of the few full-time marketers employed by large libraries specifically for this purpose – but they have their own problems, because their colleagues often fail to understand properly the importance of their work);
- all of us really should start to see marketing in a different and more relaxed light;

- everyone should feel responsible for ensuring that everything we do in the library contributes somehow to the successful promotion of our wonderful libraries.

The same marketing principles apply to all kinds of libraries – different library types don't imply different universes. When it comes to marketing methods and marketing needs, there are in fact great similarities between academic, school, public and corporate libraries. There are the same demands from all kinds of library customers, increased by the growing trends towards lifetime learning and distance studying. All kinds of libraries must learn from each other, must borrow each other's good ideas and must try to cooperate as much as possible.

# 2

# Why is marketing so important?

> Marketing is the process of planning and executing the conception, pricing, promotion, and distribution of ideas, goods, services, organizations, and events to create and maintain relationships that will satisfy individual and organizational objectives. (Boone and Kurtz, 1998)

One professional marketer with whom I discussed the concept of this book declared roundly that marketing is *not* a suitable activity for librarians!

I asked why not? Who else is going to work at marketing libraries? We cannot just sit there and hope that somebody else will do it for us. We must do it ourselves. To succeed in marketing is not a matter of luck. Everybody can contribute, but it needs a lot of work to achieve the targets. Our whole environment is more and more market-oriented, and we as customers are more and more getting acclimatised to it. We are overwhelmed by PR and marketing efforts from the cradle to the grave – literally. That is why we as librarians must maintain our presence among all these competing messages, but in our own way and sticking to our own principles.

# Does a successful operation really need any marketing?

'An excellent service doesn't need any marketing, it is self-evident.' This attitude is just not viable any more. If marketing is optional, or even unnecessary, why do we have a whole industry full of marketing people? Are they marketing only poor-quality products or unnecessary services? No, of course not. But marketing and PR take up more and more space in the economy (in some sectors the costs of marketing are even higher than the costs of making the product). This is because we have so many choices all the time, and so many agents trying to influence us to choose their product or service.

Every product, service or institution must now justify its existence – and so must libraries. We have been very fortunate in that for many years we didn't need to do this. Our activities have historically been considered to be both desirable and necessary – even essential – in universities, schools, businesses and local communities. But all this is changing now. Already our service in its current form is sometimes questioned, and where it isn't there is a serious risk that it will be in the near future. No longer is there absolute or even tacit approval from politicians – government or local – nor from university faculty, school governors or head teachers, company directors and others in key positions to influence library budgets and fundamental decisions. If we, the representatives of libraries, do not act now to demonstrate how important we are, and how significant a resource we constitute for the whole of society, we will just not be noticed in the ongoing information flow.

Most other sectors put enormous resources into marketing. Each piece of advertising they put out, each brochure, each campaign costs a lot of money. There are many different estimates and ways of calculating the cost, but it is not unusual to find a marketing budget of 10 per cent of total turnover. There are businesses where it is 50 per cent, and even more. How much of your library annual expenditure goes towards marketing efforts? It would be interesting to see this figure, *if* you have any chance of finding it.

Most probably the figure, whatever it is, does not even start to approach that of other activities. Is it so surprising, then, that libraries get so little recognition any more when they get so little space in daily newspapers and on TV? Of course the library just doesn't have the same financial resources as many other sectors. So it is vital that we find other ways of tackling the challenge. But we also need to be brave enough to use at least part of our budget for marketing. Maybe it is time for some redistribution of expenditure?

We must all get involved in marketing, even those of us in the library who have no relevant experience or who don't find it easy to relate to the concept. It is not enough to have just one very dedicated marketing person at the library, who may be very good and can probably draw nice pictures – everybody working at the library needs to contribute to this process.

> Romeo and Juliet didn't die of broken hearts, they died because of lack of communication. (Anon.)

We all believe sincerely that we are doing important and meaningful work, but do our customers know about it? Do we communicate it to them in the most effective way – one which gets through to them and which they can understand? We need to be aware of the crucial importance of promoting our message.

A project to make the library more visible is not often at the top of our priority list, and it gets lost among the other more traditional things we prefer doing. But if we continue to keep our heads firmly buried in the sand, won't the rest of our community start to believe that in the long run we are not as important as other public, academic or commercial facilities? Maybe they could organise the information they need in a different way? Wouldn't that be absurd, when we know absolutely as professionals that we can do it best, and that we are by far the most knowledgeable in the information field?

To put it simply, if all librarians are properly involved in the marketing effort, the probability increases that the library will stay strong, and that our profession will keep its leading role in information provision.

We have to tell people that we exist, and what we can achieve for them. This we can do in many different ways, depending on our local environment, beliefs and practices. That's why we must involve marketing routines in our daily work. We must always think marketing.

To be successful in marketing it is very important that everyone is aware of the need and has plenty of ideas, but even more important is to follow up these ideas and put them into practice in a properly coordinated way. Just as in a play in the theatre, where all the actors have different roles but follow a common script, there must be a marketing script. This is normally called a marketing plan. Within this plan there is naturally the assumption, or at least the realistic hope, that everyone will run in the same direction and that accordingly the target will be reached. To integrate marketing in this way into the totality of library routines is often the most difficult part of the project. To minimise the problems and difficulties it usually helps to start on a small scale, and gradually to involve more and more routines. We cannot expect any monumental changes as soon as we start our marketing efforts; successful results will not come overnight, because marketing takes time and needs total commitment.

## Marketing involves development

> *Tempora mutantur et nos mutamur in illis* – The times are changing, and we are changing with them.

A most valuable by-product of marketing is that it can be a very efficient way of developing and fine-tuning the work carried out in the library. The thought processes we have to go through provide a continual check that we are on the right track in our primary activities.

We can often be enthusiastic during the planning stage, whereas putting something fundamentally new into practice is much more intimidating. It is quite natural to prefer to hang on to what we have and to fear the unknown.

That times are changing is nothing new, of course, but everything happens much more rapidly now, especially in the information business. All kinds of marketing are ongoing processes, many of which will never be fully completed as originally planned because changing circumstances mean that they have to be reviewed and updated all the time. We have to repeat our mantra constantly in order to achieve results. Sometimes we need to find new solutions for the same problem, as our environment develops and as our customers, and the rest of the community with which we have to interact, are changing their ways of working too.

It hardly needs saying that everyone working on development and marketing will meet difficulties and problems. Probably, in spite of all our good intentions, we will not be received with open arms by all our colleagues, nor will people love our ideas first time out, and maybe not even the second or third time. Then again, we can be wrong-footed because, for example, the senior managers or politicians who ultimately control our futures sometimes change jobs, and then we have to start all over again. But this is what life is like in all other businesses, and so it is for us in libraries. Most marketing departments find it hard to run in the same direction all the time and to get understanding and sympathy from their colleagues and senior management, but this doesn't mean that one can dispense with marketing. We should just be aware that there will probably be some problems.

All economics textbooks all around the world say that competition is good, useful, formative and leads a business forward. So surely this must apply even to the library. Let us therefore use our competition and learn from the world around us.

There was a time when it was impossible to locate books, let alone their content, without some knowledge of classification systems and cataloguing rules. Today people can track down most information through the internet – both the things you want to obtain, and unfortunately also sometimes material which is disturbing and which you would prefer to avoid. Information can be sought by free text searching, or via search engines like Yahoo! or by exploiting other techniques and tools which are totally different from the traditional methods of the library professional. It can be hard for us to accept that often the new techniques are more effective than those with which the older among us were brought up.

Many people in our profession are rather sceptical about any services which were not developed by librarians for libraries, especially when they find patrons are actually using such devices in their libraries. They deplore this sort of activity as searching just for the sake of searching. Some of us do tend to think that our professional portals are what should be used in the first instance, even though in our heart of hearts we know that they are obsolescent for most purposes and no one else is going to use them. We just have to accept that the first choice for most people is Google. (According to *The Charleston Report* (2007), Google is still the leader of the ten top websites.) The fundamental point here is that we must listen to our customers and understand how they think, and then respond accordingly and not try to overrule them with our own beliefs. If our customers are going to use Google (or other search engines), we must start from that point.

Furthermore, Google and its relations are coming closer and closer to the library world with developments like Google Scholar.

> John Regazzi, managing director of market development at Elsevier, described studies that show that 70 percent of professionals use the Internet constantly in their work (and even of those over the age of 55, 90% use it six or seven times each week). When Elsevier researchers asked librarians and scientists to name their top three most reliable online services, librarians named ScienceDirect, ISI's Web of Science, and Medline.

Scientists, on the other hand, named Google, Yahoo and PubMed. (Quoted by Tenopir, 2004)

## Do we really need libraries any more?

Henry Ford's reputation was as an opponent of all design tricks and changes, and his famous slogan was 'You can have your Model T in any colour so long as it's black'. This was supposedly because black paint was fast-drying and for that reason it suited the conveyor belt best. But even the great Henry Ford had to change his mind and start to produce cars in other colours, because that was what his competitors were offering.

Let us learn from history (and be better than Henry Ford, even if he thought history was bunk), and as soon as possible let us start trying out new colours and new services in our library offerings. 'If you can't beat them, join them' is appropriate even for the library world. All these new technological developments open up a lot of opportunities for libraries, and we must keep our eyes open to take advantage of them.

Today's scientists and schoolchildren can usually find the first lead for information on their own. Where we librarians can contribute is with help at the next stage, by asking the right questions, evaluating sources and extracting what our customers need from the enormous amount of information available.

There will be in the future a very substantial need for human filters and selectors – the role we are best qualified to fill. The consensus in our professional world is of course that libraries will be needed more then ever. But even so we have to recognise that we must help each other to project ourselves as the necessary partners which we undoubtedly are, and to market ourselves and the things we are good at.

# The courage to drop something

Marketing costs both money and time. And usually we don't have either of them. What can we do, then? The answer is as simple as it is unpleasant and difficult to digest.

Cut out some of your activities, even drop some of the services you are currently providing, and you will find that you obtain the time and money for marketing.

The sad reality is that we will not get any more money or more staff or other resources until we do something positive and interesting. Unless we can demonstrate that we have more users or new customer groups, we will never get more money. But we are also very preoccupied with our ordinary work: 'We really want to do something, but we just don't have the time' is the refrain heard far too often in the library world. But what if we are devoting too much of our effort in the wrong direction? There is probably some truth in this, so we must constantly scrutinise our activities with almost brutal honesty in order to determine what is really important and what we must get rid of.

To take an example from Covey (1989), suppose you were to come upon someone in the woods who is working feverishly trying to saw down a tree.

'What are you doing?' you ask.

'Can't you see?' comes the impatient reply. 'I'm cutting down this tree.'

'You look exhausted!' you exclaim. 'How long have you been at it?'

'Over five hours,' he returns, 'and I'm worn out! This is hard work.'

'Well, why don't you take a break for a few minutes and sharpen that saw?' you enquire. 'I'm sure it would make the job a lot faster.'

'I don't have time to sharpen the saw,' the man says emphatically. 'I'm too busy trying to cut this tree down!'

Sharpening the saw is about renewing ourselves – physically, mentally, spiritually and emotionally.

Those of us who are working in a library need to stop for a while, and to put more effort into marketing. To make the time to do that we almost certainly have to drop something we are doing now. I do not want to disparage all the work that is currently carried out in libraries, and all the things which we absolutely have to do each day, but we must actively create more time for marketing if we want to reach out with our message.

Is everything we do on a daily basis really necessary? What happens if we cut out some minor activity? I believe that if once we start this thought process, it is not all that frightening or strange. Any of us can spot something which isn't absolutely necessary. But of course everything must be discussed and planned and coordinated. One move which frees up half an hour a day for someone generates over two free hours a week, and that is a good beginning. These hours can be used for thinking through and developing marketing ideas.

We can ask if there are any happy outcomes from eliminating tasks. Of course there are, especially if we are then able to take on new and more interesting work and as a result we get the opportunity to influence the library's activities in a positive way. Better to forestall than to be forestalled. When we have been successful at first analysing our activities, next at getting rid of some of them, then at starting to develop an initial strategy for marketing, that is when we are on the right track.

So you should aim to start with something small, then go back and evaluate whether the decision to eliminate this activity was right or wrong. Even if in the worst-case scenario it turns out that a lot of customers are likely to be affected adversely by this decision, is it really such a catastrophe? Probably not, because it was only a minor change and we can easily reverse it. Think again, and find something else. Eventually you will find the right things that can be cut out without problematical consequences.

'Kill your darlings' was the best advice I was ever given when I started my own consultancy. This is a great dictum, but one that is very hard to follow. I am convinced that most of us find it very difficult to pension off our own brilliant ideas, those concepts we have had for a long time and with which we have a personal relationship – almost a responsibility for. But ideas are getting old just as we are, and the world around is changing too, so maybe these ideas don't have a meaningful place any more?

In my own experience, what I had always thought was a fantastic idea often proved over time to be just not good enough. On the other hand an idea from someone else – it could be from my boss, a colleague, my children, my husband or even a customer or competitor – turns out to be the right one.

We have just got to accept that this can happen – and then learn to take advantage of it. Personal prestige is nowhere near as important as following the best concepts, whatever their origin may be.

During this process we will almost certainly have to change our way of thinking, and maybe even change ourselves a little. To arrive at the insight that after all something is not such a good thing to do doesn't mean that the original idea was wrong. Maybe it is just not suitable for this occasion or in this environment.

Do we really have to abandon all our traditional thinking and activities? Maybe not all of them, but we must do something – possibly only changing some things instead of dropping them completely, if a case can be made for some level of retention. It can be very stimulating and good for the soul to change our way of seeing problems, but what hard work it is and how very painful! That fantastic idea which I have treasured for 20 years must now be sacrificed because the world has changed and there are now too many arguments against it. If we want to develop ourselves and our organisations, we must sometimes abandon our brilliant ideas from former times, and that is when the real creativity comes in.

You have probably heard that the Chinese character for chaos is the same as that for opportunity. Well, that is just Chinese, you may say. But how about if we could change the way we think in our very structured world, and by so doing we could bring a little more chaos into our way of thinking? If we could 'think outside the box', as the management books term it? Chaos seems dangerous, but remember that the world around us really is chaotic, and unexpected things keep cropping up. Chaos could work as a catalyst: we will get used to it and it will not paralyse us. Instead, once we have passed the first difficult stage it will bring a lot of creativity.

# Problems are only opportunities in working clothes!

There are many problem situations that we are afraid to tackle in an innovative way because right from the start we assume that you just cannot do that sort of thing. Maybe nobody in our library, or so far as we know anywhere else in the library world, has ever done it before. This is of course a completely unnecessary and negative outlook. Thinking like this can lead to lots of good initiatives being stifled just because we are fearful of an uncertain outcome.

What would happen if we were to bypass some unwritten rules or trespass on some invisible territory marks in our workplace (naturally I am talking about those which will not create any ethical or legal consequences)? You would be surprised: mostly nothing awful would result! And so what if anything did happen – would it really matter? We can't always be that clever, nor can we have the perfect solution for every single problem which crops up; sometimes even a half-baked idea is better than no idea at all. The worst that can happen is that we get some negative criticism for some of our ideas. Instead, think of what we have to gain if the new concept works out – so why not be a bit bold today for a change?

The strong predisposition towards self-criticism, which is so typical in librarians, holds us back in many situations. We are too often inclined to begin by emphasising all the negatives. But think again, and remember how often we just don't have the time or the energy to highlight the positives as well. We tend to raise the bar so high that some things can never be achieved successfully in our eyes.

At one training session, on the topic of how to perform successfully in front of a large audience, the course leader hardly even acknowledged some negative comments made early on by a few delegates about their colleagues; he focused instead on all the positive and constructive aspects that had been raised. After that nobody brought up anything negative; everyone was concentrating on the up side and put all the emphasis there instead. The focus was on the need for change and on the best direction for it.

To change your business is not easy, and it needs a lot of new thinking and training. We must practise in order to develop the ability to market ourselves. It is the same as when you are starting to learn a new language; you just wouldn't dream of trying to present a lecture in the new language after nothing more than a quick preliminary look through the grammar book. Practice brings skills as well as confidence in one's ability.

## Is there such a thing as bad PR?

In general terms, as long as people are talking about us in any way at all it is beneficial from a marketing point of view. The reverse is that when there is complete silence on the subject of our library and its staff then there is serious cause for concern. As they say, almost any publicity is good publicity.

Exposure in a bad light is not something we should strive for. On the other hand it is important that libraries are talked about in the public domain – of course not at any cost, but I often think we exaggerate the potential harm from possible negative publicity. It goes without saying that we shouldn't actively get involved in negative situations, but nor should we be afraid of new things which just might create negative perceptions. We must weigh the pros and cons in every case.

One way or another, I think the old saying that all media exposure is good advertising is correct. For example, I was once having breakfast when my attention was forcibly drawn to a newspaper article which had a picture of one of my colleagues; he was standing with a very sad face in front of his empty periodical shelves. But in the middle of the article he was quoted as saying: 'The use of periodicals has sky-rocketed – this would never have happened without the internet.' The rather boring photograph probably attracted not only me but lots of other people to read about libraries. I think that is great.

As librarians we are not familiar with the process of discussing the problems and dangers of marketing. On the other hand, we are very comfortable when discussing and evaluating our manager's orders, or the politics of cultural foundations, and so on. We willingly sign up to petitions for good causes. However, when it comes to entering what seems to us to be the foreign territory of advertising, or public relations and dealing with the media, we tend to be frightened at the possibility that we might do something wrong – or even break the law. Librarians tend to stick to the law even before any law has been passed. So when we have something important to say – something which really must be put over forcefully for our message to succeed – we are reluctant to be positive, let alone aggressive. In most countries there is a law to protect the public along the lines of the UK Trade Descriptions Act; but so long as what you say in any advertisement is truthful, there is no risk of breaching the regulations.

## Difficulties with giving and receiving negative responses

It is always hard for you as a librarian to market yourself and your institution. It can also feel very uncomfortable and out of character to take the risk of getting an unfavourable response. On the other hand, this is probably the only thing we do risk – the possibility of getting a 'no'. Is this potential 'no' really all that dangerous? It can be much more unpleasant to have your budget cut, or some of your branches closed. This sort of thing is already an unpleasant fact of life for many of us. That is why we must dare to pose the difficult question, why we must dare to wait for the answer, and most importantly why we must get used to taking the risk of getting turned down. The risk involved in asking, compared with that of not asking, is no more than the possibility of a negative, and then the worst-case scenario is that we are back at square one as if we had never asked the question. We all know that we can never expect a 'yes' if we never ask. So, what are we waiting for?

Our frequent reluctance to risk exposing ourselves reminds me of the story of Mrs Owen, who was going to borrow some sugar from her neighbour. On her way round next door she began to remember that the two of them really didn't know each other that well. 'And maybe she won't be at home. And even if she is at home maybe she won't have any sugar. And even she has got some, maybe she will think that I am too pushy...' Finally she got there and managed to pluck up the courage to knock at the neighbour's door. But when the neighbour opened the door all Mrs Owen could say was: 'And you know what – you can keep your damn sugar to yourself!'

# 3

# Marketing tools

I hope that by this stage most readers are convinced that marketing is not only desirable but also possible if we are to increase the chances of survival and success for libraries and librarians. A very helpful route to get started towards achieving this necessary improvement is by using some of the numerous marketing tools which are available. There are many different models, theories and strategies, and they come and go depending on things like the shape of the business environment and the changes within it. Some theories are popular and widely used for a while, and then sometimes fade away, only to come to life again a few years later. I have tried out several of these in my marketing courses, and also in more in-depth practical work at many libraries. Actually, in my experience it really doesn't matter which model of analysis or strategy you choose. Stick with the first one you select for a while, and see how it works. If it is not successful, use another one. In any event I strongly recommend that you try using one or more of the standard marketing tools I outline below to provide a framework for your thinking and planning – I have found all of them very appropriate for library activities.

If we are to think and plan coherently it is absolutely vital for all of us to understand the entirety, the total context of all the work we are doing and the services we provide. It is only when this understanding is achieved that all of us in the library will be driven to work along the same lines, when the various different departments appreciate better what the others are trying to achieve.

Basic experience and intuition are very important, and they should be combined with the various textbook techniques. The latter will help to make it easier to start the process – again for the entire library.

In my opinion it is easiest to divide marketing activities into four steps, both for individual staff and for the whole library: analysis, strategy, implementation and feedback.

# Analysis

This process is the audit of an organisation and its environment before starting the marketing exercise. It helps us to focus on the key issues. It shows us what we need to do, and gives us a complete picture of the current situation; also it helps us to see all the different aspects, especially when all staff are working in the same mode. In fact, analysis should be continuous and should feed all the aspects of planning. It is very important to be almost brutally honest when carrying out the analysis. We must avoid the danger of seeing things as we think they should be and not as they really are. Sometimes we are going to be surprised at what we discover, and sometimes it is not all that pleasant to have to recognise that we or our colleagues are not really performing as well as we hoped and believed. But again, it is vital to be honest.

Which model you use for analysis is of course your own decision. One of the best known is SWOT.

## *SWOT*

This is a technique for analysis which is very widely used in the commercial world and which also works very well for libraries. Here we monitor our strengths, weaknesses, opportunities and threats (Figure 3.1).

The top two squares describe the current situation and the internal factors. The lower two describe how things will be in the future, and the external factors. Here are some typical examples of each element.

- Strengths
  - specialist expertise
  - reputation for reliability.
- Weaknesses
  - lack of marketing experience
  - budget cuts
  - inappropriate organisation.
- Opportunities
  - a new product or service (e.g. e-resources)
  - new customer groups.
- Threats
  - competitors (internet, Google)
  - technical problems.

**Figure 3.1** SWOT analysis

| strengths | weaknesses |
|---|---|
| opportunities | threats |

If you want go further, or if you have gone through the SWOT process several times and feel it no longer provides the right challenge, there are other models to try out, like PEST.

## PEST

PEST is a way of evaluating political, economic, socio-cultural and technological factors.

### Political factors

The political arena has a huge influence upon the regulation of businesses, and on the spending power of consumers and other businesses; it obviously also impacts on libraries. You must consider issues such as:

- what does the political environment look like?
- how stable is it?
- what is the university/local authority/company view on marketing?

### Economic factors

- What will the economy look like for the next three years?
- What are the prospects for our budgets, and for inflation?
- How do we see the employment situation in our industry?
- Property trends – will our library rent etc. change?

### Socio-cultural factors

The social and cultural influences on libraries vary from country to country, but it is very important that such factors are considered.

- What are our society's attitudes to library products and services?
- What are the roles of men and women within society?
- What are the demographics, and demographic trends?
- Do our users have strong or weak opinions on library issues?
- What are the level of education and the attitude to information of our owners?

## Technological factors

Technology is becoming more and more important, so let us look at the following points.

- How do the government and our own hierarchy view technology?
- How fast is the relevant technology moving forward?
- Can we manage on our own or do we need outside expertise?
- Are any new products that are becoming available less costly than their predecessors, and will they provide better quality?
- Will the new technologies offer our customers innovative products and services?
- How may the distribution of information be changed by new technologies, e.g. books and journals via the internet?

## *Porter's five forces analysis*

Another technique that is often effective is Porter's five forces analysis. This process for analysis and business strategy was developed by Michael E. Porter in 1979. It looks at the business and general environment from the competitive point of view. It may seem an unlikely avenue for libraries, as we tend to believe that we don't really have any competitors. Yet it can often be worthwhile to think again on this issue, and to have a closer look. We need to monitor current or prospective competitors and substitutes (e.g. Google), and also:

- the threat of entry
- the power of the customer
- the power of suppliers
- the threat of substitutes
- competitive rivalry.

## The threat of entry

- Is it at all likely that completely new actors might come into our library world?
- How loyal are our customers likely to be in this event?
- Might any new entrants get support from our governing body?

## The power of customers

- Could our customers feel so powerful that at some time in the future they might try to force us to offer much more in the way of products or services than we do at present, or could they even demand the impossible and so threaten our very existence? This risk is typically high where there are a few large players in a market, e.g. the major grocery chains.
- Are our service and quality good enough?

## The power of suppliers

- Is the suppliers' position strong?
- Do any of them have a monopoly?
- Could they force us into something we really do not want to do, or try to make us go in a direction which our customers are not pressing for – like switching from one software supplier to another?
- Are we important to our suppliers?

## The threat of substitutes

- Is it at all likely that some less expensive or more efficient substitute for our services and products might emerge?

## Competitive rivalry

- How many competitors do we have?
- Could they work together, or merge and so become stronger?
- Or can we really believe that it still going to be true that no one else can do what we do? If this is definitely the case then we have enormous strength.

# Strategy – the marketing focus

In order to choose the right strategy, and which products and services we want to market, it helps to use a matrix. Matrices are used for studying what a market looks like, both currently and in the future.

## *Boston matrix*

Personally, I prefer the Boston matrix, a technique that was created by Bruce Henderson for the Boston Consulting Group in 1970. This is because it suits very well our need to monitor our routines, products and services. We can with its help rank these products and services on the basis of their relative market shares and growth rates.

Let's have a look at each individual product or service and place it on to the matrix. These are some examples I have come across at my courses, and of course they do not necessarily apply to your library. Each library is different, and these are just examples.

- *Dogs*. These are the products or services which have only a low share of a low-growth market. We must seriously consider getting rid of these in order to find time, space and funding for new and better offerings. Some examples for public libraries might be the library archive, any official literature which is stored but never accessed, and most CD-ROMs. For university libraries examples might be print reference collections,

CD-ROMs (like archival data, newspapers, etc.), exchanges with other libraries and dissertations in other European languages. And for all libraries throughout the world, those long and inefficient internal meetings with too many staff, most of them not properly prepared. We must have only the appropriate people and only at the right meeting!

- *Milk cows.* These are items with a high share of a slow-growth market. They are excellent, but only for the time being. Examples for some public libraries would be books, films and information services (at least in their current shape); and for some university libraries photocopy collections and short-loan material, printed help guides and workbooks, and reference books.

- *Question marks or problem children.* These are the products or services which consume resources and generate little in return, but which could change for the better in the future. Some examples for public libraries would be e-books, or how the media mix will develop; and for university libraries certain portals and many new technologies, e-books, webpages and guides, and legacy VLEs (virtual learning environments). Another problem child for university libraries may be the so-called Big Deals: online aggregations of journals that publishers offer as a one-price, one-size-fits-all package. In a Big Deal, libraries agree to buy electronic access to all of a commercial publisher's journals for a price based on current payments to that publisher, plus some increment. Under the terms of the contract, annual price increases are capped for a number of years (Frazier, 2001).

- *Stars.* These are the ones with high market growth and which are easy to maintain. You must do everything to preserve and build your stars. For some public libraries these may include audio books, thrillers, student literature and space for reading and studying; and for university libraries e-journals, repositories, intranets, courses and workshops.

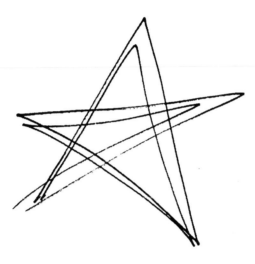

Using the Boston matrix is an easy and effective way of monitoring our products and services. The process immediately forces us to answer some key questions. Should we really keep those services and products which are not that important to that many users? Can we rationalise them? Is the offering which used to be a star really still a star, or has it become a dog?

Try to find dogs. What will happen if we cut out this service, or stop buying this product? Also remember that even products or services which are not stars, but which are not conspicuous failures either, are still consuming energy and space and general resources, and most probably consume more than they warrant. If on the other hand we eliminate them it will free our resources and energy for something else more important. We *need* to find dogs, so that we can cut out some routines and stop trying to do everything. We will suffer serious damage if we go on trying to be all things to all people, and if we attempt to keep up all the old routines along with all the new ones. As I have said, we librarians are typically afraid to receive a negative response when we ask a question, but at the same time we don't like to refuse a request either, and so gradually an unnecessary workload builds up.

There are also some other matrix approaches for developing our market strategy.

## Ansoff's matrix

One approach which has wide respect is Ansoff's matrix, developed by Igor Ansoff in 1957. I have found it generally less appropriate for library strategy than Boston, but I have seen it work effectively in some environments. It focuses on four key ways of achieving growth.

- *Market penetration.* This involves increasing the sales of a current service or product, and penetrating its market in greater depth, either by heavy promotion or by reducing prices. Price is not nearly so relevant in our environment as in the commercial world, but we can give some products more promotion in order to draw attention to their merits. For example, we can promote some portals at the expense of others.

- *Product development.* Here the organisation aims to develop new products targeted at the current market, in the expectation that they will gain more sales and market share. So we could replace any services which are very time-consuming and maybe very expensive with others which are more economical.

- *Market development.* This strategy is built around selling existing products into new markets. This can be done either via careful market analysis and segmentation, to try to locate new and different purchasers of the product, or alternatively by selling the product to new geographical markets. Through market development we could find new customers for our existing products, or maybe we could explore how we might assist in our owner marketing with these products.

- *Diversification.* This involves a fundamental change in your core activities towards providing something new, for example by moving away from offering print copies of some journals towards providing online versions only.

Beyond these four strategies, a final option libraries may consider is consolidation. Here an organisation decides to withdraw from some of its current markets or to eliminate some of its current offerings; it scales back on operations generally while still selling some of its existing products in existing markets. The most obvious application is for us to stop doing *everything* and have the courage to eliminate some offerings (see p. 13).

## Four Ps

Yet another technique to help develop a strategy is the 'Four Ps': product, place, promotion and price (see www.netmba.com).

- *Product.* The product is the totality of the offering of goods and services to the potential customer. This includes its look, how it is to be used and even its packaging, and also any support provided or other intangibles which the customer will receive. What does our product or service look like? Is it something which is easy to use and understand? At this stage we decide what kind of products we will buy in for our customers, and what kind of services we will offer.

- *Place.* This is where and how your product is distributed. Are you going to provide it yourself directly, or indirectly through a distributor or some other middle-man? If it is a service, will you deliver it in person, or through the internet or by telephone? These questions all involve 'place'. For libraries this will include the physical location – is it good enough, or could it practicably be changed for the better? Here we should also consider a question which is posed later in the book, that of 'going out' from the library and maybe marketing the librarian as well as the library itself (see p. 58).

- *Promotion.* This is the part of marketing where you are trying to create and build up demand. Sometimes a distinction is made between push and pull promotions. Advertising 'pulls' by making the potential buyer aware of your product or service and then, you hope, asking for it or at least for more information about it. Incentives, such as premiums or price reductions, 'push' your product or service by encouraging your customers to use it more often or in greater volume than they might otherwise do. How can we make our customers understand the value of the library? This is where PR and a whole range of different specific activities are called for.

- *Price.* This is of course how much you charge for your product or service. The sort of things you have to bear in mind include whether you will charge the same price all the time, or modify it in some way. Varied pricing could typically occur depending on geographical or seasonal factors, the level of competition or the volume involved. Additionally, with a service, price can be changed up or down according to the level of service offered or required.

Most libraries do not charge for most products or services, but all the same we do need to consider whether we can justify some of the costs of providing them, because in the end they determine what we can offer.

# Implementation and feedback

By this stage you should know all that is relevant about your own organisation, about the environment in which you must operate, and about your key products and services; and you have given serious thought to your marketing strategy. How are you going to take the next step of *implementation*? The next chapter on marketing in practice offers some suggestions, but *you are the experts*, you know. You have done this sort of thing pretty well in the past, and now you are ready to do it even better because you know even more about your environment – both what it looks like now and, with some educated guesses, what the future holds. The crucial thing is just to get on with it wholeheartedly. Try to share the different marketing activities in the library between yourself and all your colleagues, and write the plan down and get people to accept their roles. It is easier when they have been involved in all the earlier processes of analysis and the development of strategy.

## *Marketing plan*

Having a written plan helps people appreciate that things are moving forward. A typical comment I have had during a consultancy exercise was: 'I thought that we hadn't done anything during the autumn, but when I looked at the list I saw that we had actually achieved quite a lot.'

It is very important to make a formal note of everything you have actually completed, and don't ever forget to give each other credit for your respective achievements. A cheerful and positive atmosphere gives everyone the confidence and courage to move on to the next step and the next set of activities.

## Using feedback

Here are two examples of how *feedback* can make a real difference to the next stage.

A library invited an interesting speaker for a meeting one evening, but it didn't make enough effort to market the event effectively. In the end only three outsiders showed up. This was a catastrophe, of course, so all the staff from the library attended the meeting themselves to help make up the numbers. Because they felt so sorry for the speaker and wanted to make up for their failure, they all participated very enthusiastically and the atmosphere was very good with a lot of laughs. One of the three outside visitors was a journalist who happened to have a great deal of interest in the subject involved. He was impressed by what he saw of the library and its staff, so he wrote a series of articles which incidentally praised the library for arranging the session. The library was able to use all this in its owner marketing, and the library director cleverly exploited the fortunate outcome in a very important meeting by referring to the press coverage.

Correctly used, feedback is invaluable for the future. Even failures are very important; we just need to have the courage to see and recognise them, and not merely put our head in the sand and move on blindly into the next project.

Once a library in southern Sweden had put a lot of effort into preparing and sending out its information lists, and the staff were very disappointed when they didn't receive any reaction, so they just gave up and the project was terminated.

There is nothing wrong with terminating some projects, but on this occasion there wasn't sufficient basis for doing so because the library was not getting proper and comprehensive feedback. It never cross-examined the recipients of the lists. I am sure that if the library had done so it would have received a positive reaction, as the information was good and interesting. This library was not *proactive*, and so it let the customer take the decision inadvertently and by default – the very customer who has his own problems, has no spare time and doesn't give much thought to the library, although he likes the service it provides. If we do not proactively question what the customer thinks about this or that product or service he will *not* tell us. There is of course the exception of the few really nice customers who will show their appreciation of us anyway, but in reality to get the answers we need we must put some real effort into posing the relevant questions to users as a whole. The feedback in this case was that the library had started the process well, but just didn't follow it properly all the way through.

## Branding

> A brand is the sum total of everything a company does – the good, the bad and even the off strategy – that creates a large context or an identity in the consumer's mind. (Bedbury and Fenichell, 2002)

When somebody says Volvo, I immediately think of safe travel by car. I don't really know why I have never had a Volvo, but in my case Volvo has always been successful with its 'safety' branding. When there is so much information all around us, branding will have more and more value in helping us to distinguish between the many alternatives which are available. As with all other companies and organisations, the library is associated with a brand. Our brand is fantastic. It is positive, it is old and well established (the first library was in existence more than 4,500 years ago – see the clay tablet from the Ebla library archive at www.abu. nb.ca/ecm/pictures/2002/sept.htm), and it is generally liked by everyone and not just by our customers. I have never heard anybody say that they hated the idea of a library, or even that a library gives them bad feelings. The 'library', for better or worse, is our brand, and so we should do all we can to strengthen the positive aspects of the brand. Of course, on the other side there are some minor negative connotations as well: people may think that the library can be boring, that it does nothing for me, it is too quiet for my taste, all it does is stock books, there are too many rules – and so on.

What do we want our brand to be? Should we maybe change the name 'library' to 'learning centre' or 'information centre'? Well, I don't have the answer, but instinctively I feel that it would be a great pity to give up the 'library' brand!

However, each library must decide what it most wants to be known for. Information, the word librarians love, is maybe no longer so useful and positive because, as mentioned above, we are all being overwhelmed by information, and most people do *not* want more information. We can put people off by offering them yet more information, even if it may be more selective and so more relevant. This is possibly because the very word 'information' is no longer so inherently interesting, and it is not as specific to the library as it used to be. 'Information' is now used by every sales person, starting with telephones and ending with electricity companies. So I would recommend that we place less emphasis on the word 'information' in our marketing.

We should make a list of all the things we want *all* our customers to think about when they hear or read the word 'library':

- relevant and reliable information;
- a pleasant place to go to, or to phone or contact through the internet (we have more than just physical visitors);
- help.

What I mean when I say '*all* our customers' includes the customers who have never been in the library yet, but who still have good feelings about the *brand*.

When I visited the Library of Congress for the first of maybe two dozen visits, I met a librarian there who told me that he often gets questions like 'What do you do in the library all day?', and 'What is a library useful for, if you are not studying, or searching for something special or if you don't have some particular interest? Why is a library needed? Who actually needs a library?' Well, these are questions I am sure we all hear from time to time, even if we maybe don't get them personally.

My friend from the Library of Congress used to tell an old story which everyone understood (I mention that because we sometimes talk to an audience outside the library while we are still thinking in our 'library language', which is not always that easy for laymen to understand). Anyway, he talked about how when NASA sent the first man to the moon, everything scientific was almost ready except that they didn't know how to design a space suit. So NASA asked the Library of Congress to send them copies of all the Buck Rogers comics, because Buck Rogers had been on the moon around 1930, and he was of course wearing a space suit. From these comics NASA got the necessary inspiration, and so designed the first space suit for Neil Armstrong.

Well, you probably all have much better stories from your own daily library life, but I have never forgotten this one, and I always connect it with the Library of Congress. The branding of the Library of Congress means that I can easily use this anecdote whenever I want to explain something about libraries and how they can fulfil any information need, and also how it pays to *store* information.

## The fine art of negotiation

All marketing activities involve some kind of negotiation, so it is important for us to be prepared for this and especially to understand the psychology which underlies the process.

Rhonda Abrams (2007) has some interesting insights into this topic. She points out that in all aspects of life we are negotiating. We negotiate when we are at work – whether it's with suppliers, customers, our boss or our staff. We negotiate with our family members – over big and small things. We negotiate whenever we buy or sell something.

Most of us think of negotiations as 'zero-sum' games – what one side gives up, the other gets, and vice versa. Maybe that is true if you are never going to do business with, live with or be friends with the person on the other side again. This is the transaction view of negotiations.

For most of us, however, negotiations are just one aspect of ongoing alliances. You are still going to be buying from your supplier, you still want to use your mechanic and you still want to have a pleasant dinner with your spouse. In these negotiations we recognise that, sure, we want to get what we want or need. But the other person had better feel that he or she is being treated fairly, too. That is the relationship view of negotiations.

Negotiations are far more likely to succeed when both sides share the same attitude. For instance, if both parties in a negotiation are transaction-oriented, the negotiation may get heated, but everyone is likely to understand that it is just part of the process and so will not take it personally. And if both parties are relationship-oriented they are almost certain to be able to reach an amicable and fair agreement. One side may have to give up something more today, but the other party will be willing to give up something more tomorrow. Both parties are able to take the long view, recognising that the relationship itself has value.

The worst negotiations are when the two parties have differing viewpoints. If one side is concentrating solely on the transaction (what's in it for me?) while the other is also concerned about the relationship (what's best for both of us in the long run?), it's a recipe for anger, frustration and probably a long-drawn-out and unpleasant negotiation.

The best negotiators recognise the value of approaching their negotiations from a relationship point of view. After all, it's very costly and time-consuming to have to find new suppliers, let alone new customers. The best personal relationships are built on that approach, too.

In our library world we have some freedom in choosing our suppliers, so we do have options in selecting our negotiating style with them – but it must be best to go for suppliers who have the same style as ourselves. However, when we deal with our owners we are inevitably generally in a weaker position, so we have to accept that the best outcome will emerge if we adapt our style to theirs.

# Relationship marketing

A modern way of taking a view of marketing is to have a look at our interactions with all our different customers. This is called 'relationship marketing'.

According to Evert Gummesson (2002), a leading expert in relationship marketing, all employees are at least to some extent marketers, either full or part time. There are some whose main occupation is marketing, but all the other employees should be involved in marketing: 'Those employees who do not influence the relationships with customers, full-time or part-time, directly or indirectly, are redundant.'

Gummesson also distinguishes between internal part-time marketers and external marketers. These 'external marketers' can be our customers or suppliers, the media or other interested parties. It is very significant to note that these external marketers are working free of charge for us. We should use them as much as possible. The disadvantage is, of course, that we cannot really influence and direct in detail all the messages they communicate. But it shouldn't frighten us into avoiding the support they can provide – rather the opposite, we should always have these external marketers in mind and remember how much (with our guidance, however discreet) they can help us, and we must give them plenty of reasons why they should do so.

# 4

# Marketing in practice

## Owner marketing

Our owner marketing is the part which targets the 'owners', the senior people, the decision-takers at universities – our highest bosses, so to speak. It is vital to remember that this aspect of marketing is crucial, and at least as important as user marketing, if only because we always need understanding and support from our top management if our user marketing is going to be successful.

For both user and owner marketing we can use the same help – tables, matrices and so on. I am dividing marketing into these two parts mainly because I have seen many times that owner marketing doesn't receive the same priority as user marketing at some libraries. Sometimes it is even viewed with a certain amount of suspicion by some colleagues. We do not have many traditional routines for working on owner marketing, and for that reason it can be a little difficult to start the whole process and convince all the library employees that this is a necessary activity.

Very often it is only the director of the library who is involved in owner marketing, but all employees in an organisation should be involved in the marketing process. User marketing has a clear target in an 'outside' group, and the marketing techniques outlined previously are more obviously relevant to it. But even with owner marketing it is as important as ever to go through all the four steps: analysis, strategy, implementation and feedback.

We have to get used to being asked to justify why the library itself and its resources are so expensive. In all marketing we must of course be ready for this to crop up at any time, and we must have a good answer – depending on our market analysis, which we must complete first.

I will try to explain below that we can and must change any relaxed or dismissive attitude on the part of our top hierarchy, and why it is so important to do so. What do we want to achieve? Maybe something like this...

- To make our 'owners', the university authorities, the local politicians or the board of directors, become interested in our work and start to see the library as an asset rather than just a cost.

- To build up a closer relationship with these owners, maybe by contributing to something very significant, such as helping to promote the company, the district or the university. We can do this, for example, by providing good educational support, or offering interesting contributions and pieces of factual information before important meetings, or collecting all the positive facts about the university/company/district.

'I cannot just rush in into my vice chancellor's office and say to him: "Look, we are very good – give us more money."' This was a spontaneous reaction from one of my course delegates in England.

Yes, we can; but we cannot do this tomorrow, nor can we do it without a lot of preparatory work, without going through a thorough analysis and before choosing the right strategy. And it can take a long time to be able to proceed. Please remember that we must first *give* something to our owners before we can ask for anything back.

Think about how much time and effort an advertisement takes to produce, how well thought out they all are, how many copywriters, marketing experts, analysts and others are involved. We often think that the results are quite good, don't we? And similarly, we cannot do good marketing without a proper analysis of our customers to find out more about their needs. This takes time, as they don't usually spontaneously tell us what they want and how they want us to provide it. Or sometimes, a rather more revolutionary thought, they don't even know what they want, and very often don't have a clear picture of what a library and librarians can do for them. That's why we must take time to prepare everything thoroughly, and why we must allow enough time to reiterate our message. Many times.

I was once travelling to Oman for a meeting with the director of the Sultan Qaboos University Library. Because this was my first visit to Oman, I prepared myself very carefully. I learned that the official name of the country is the Sultanate of Oman, that it is located in south-west Asia on the south-east coast of the Arabian peninsula, and that the trip would take eight hours from Amsterdam. The weather is very warm: up to 28 degrees in winter, and even higher in summer. I also found out how Omani people dress. I was prepared for the fact that in the middle of our discussions we would possibly be interrupted, because Oman is a Muslim country and it was time for prayers. So I made myself ready with these preliminary studies, and I was fully expecting to meet a rather different library from those I had visited in Europe or North America.

In spite of it being such a different country (compared with Sweden or Europe or even the USA), I found it surprisingly easily to establish plenty of rapport with the librarians there, and it was less problematic to talk to them than I sometimes found it was to talk to Swedish university management or local politicians about library issues.

I think we very often wrongly assume that our own hierarchy are the same as we are, that they think as we do and have the same priorities. We live in the same country, we usually wear the same kinds of clothes, so we must therefore have the same perspectives on life and the same goals.

Well, we just have to realise that this is not always the way, and at the very least we cannot assume that it is so. We need to be very sharp and to listen very carefully; we need to analyse what our direct bosses or owners mean when they say what they want, and sometimes unfortunately we must be intuitive about what they really want and what they are not telling us. It is not at all certain or obvious that they are going to want the same things as we do, or that they have the same goals and needs as our own or those of our user customers. Their individual understanding of the issues involved is maybe not only different from ours but may also vary from the official line or from that we might reasonably expect. Or it could be a combination of all these. Bear all this in mind, and use it in order to give yourself the best chance of reaching them with the right message.

Remember that everything we use more obviously in user marketing – all the tables, analyses, matrices and other planning tools – can also be used very successfully for owner marketing purposes.

What happens if, in spite of all this preparatory work, something goes wrong when we finally make our first major owner marketing move? Maybe we prepared an hour-long presentation and only got halfway through when an urgent phone call distracted the owner, which meant that we never got the chance to finish...

Well, first we must remember that we have given it 'our best shot', at least for a first attempt. We have learned to use all the help that the textbook tables and matrices provide, so it will go much better next time. Meanwhile, practice will make us better, and there are plenty of opportunities for low-level owner marketing – for instance, coffee breaks with other departments, telephone, mail and so on. Share with your colleagues whatever scope you find for an entry channel to the decision-makers, and keep on trying out new routes.

I have a very good example from a public library in southern Sweden, which tried out what I think was a very innovative idea. The staff compiled an interesting report about how access to culture and knowledge affects physical and mental health. There were many references to other published scientific reports, but their own report was short, easy to understand and even funny. This report was greatly appreciated. It is very significant that in this case nobody had requested the report, but the library had discovered that the health of local inhabitants would be a major issue at the next regional authority meeting. The director of the library was not supposed to attend the meeting, but as she had 'this interesting and short report' she was asked to deliver it personally. She got plenty of follow-up questions and thanks, and she was asked to attend the next monthly meeting in the hope that she would bring another interesting report about whatever was the next issue to be discussed.

Of course this initiative helped the library. The message is: do not wait until you are needed – rather make yourself needed today.

Other possible ways to approach and learn more about your hierarchy or owners include:

- compiling everything that newspapers and magazines write about them over a certain period;
- giving them all kinds of data, such as historical, scientific or law reports, which relate to their individual hobby-horses;

- offering statistics they could use (the existence of which they may be entirely ignorant of);

- thinking of your training courses and trying to adapt them so they may suit your owners as well – this is an opportunity to learn more about them;

- feeding to the media snippets of news about how enthusiastic local politicians or the university hierarchy are about the sharing of more knowledge.

One very good opportunity for marketing is if you are lucky enough to rebuild or renovate your library. Usually people are very interested in anything to do with new buildings or new furniture and equipment, and we should exploit this interest. The problem is that when we are going through a process like this we are busy with other things, so we do not have time to make a real marketing plan, let alone to follow it up. Try very hard to do it anyway – this is a golden opportunity which will never repeat itself.

Keep an eye on all the reports and investigations about the services provided by the local authority or the university. Usually libraries get very favourable comments. But it is not enough just to receive a good official judgement; it must be properly used. It can be very useful in our owner marketing – otherwise there is a risk that a report which may be flattering about the library will soon be forgotten and sink without trace. Do not let people forget. This first step to self-promotion can be hard for some of us, because we are not used to taking it. And as I have said so often before, our community seems to have some kind of strange fear of receiving a 'no'. For this reason we sometimes don't even get to first base with any new and as yet unapproved and untried activities.

I make no apology for repeating that a 'no' does not mean no for always, it only means no for the present. We can always try again. Each journey starts with one step. We cannot achieve anything if we are cowardly and don't dare to take it.

The precise steps needed of course depend on each particular library situation – what kind of library is involved and so on. But one universal rule must be that owner marketing is not the job of the library director alone. 'So should all my staff run into the vice chancellor's office and try to talk about how good we are?' The answer to this question is 'No, of course not'. We need coordination and planning, but each employee at the library has a role to play in this work. Good ideas sometimes come from an unexpected direction. Results can't be expected overnight, and we need to help each other to maintain progress in the right direction. It can be difficult to identify at the start exactly what wants doing at the later stages. For this reason the most important thing is to take the initial steps you can see clearly, and then review and adjust your plans as necessary throughout the whole process.

Educate your owners by showing them what you have in your library and what the library can do for them. It is not enough to tell them this once or even twice. All these messages must be repeated many times, as in any other marketing process. We need to be very persistent and never to be put off by any lack of initial reaction to our approach.

Maybe we can get somebody within the parent body to say something positive about our activity? We all are vain and hungry for any kind of praise. We all feel that we don't get as much approval as we deserve. Think about all the politicians, the university chancellors and board directors; all these people are in very vulnerable positions, and they have to compromise and arbitrate between different demands and different people. How often do you think they hear any praise for their performance and activities? Not very often, I am sure. Why not to try to find something positive which has been said (or if necessary even say it yourself) about what they are doing? I am not saying go and be obviously sycophantic. The important thing is to find anything positive and to develop it – and most of all to find it in the first place. Marketing analysis and marketing strategy will help you to find the best route for owner marketing and the right methods for it.

'If we don't grumble we will never receive any money' – another comment from a delegate at a marketing course in Sweden. Think about it, and consider who you yourself prefer to listen to – the one who grumbles or the one who comes in with something positive and interesting. The answer is so obvious, and yet still we sometimes *start* our owner marketing by just grumbling and criticising, without any constructive suggestions. It is very important not to get stuck in this rut and instead at least to start with something forward-looking and constructive. We are sometimes too afraid of the word 'sycophant', and for that reason we do not exploit what are genuinely praiseworthy situations.

Let me illustrate the way I am thinking.

A little dog comes to a room which is full of mirrors. The dog becomes afraid and shows his teeth. Immediately all the dogs round him show their teeth as well. Imagine now what happens if the dog waves his tail instead? If we are really honest, sometimes we all behave like the little dog. But we can change that with a bit of practice.

## We are each other's customers

*The customer is always right.*

In owner marketing there is another important factor that we must always bear in mind: nothing good can be achieved in a library riddled by internal politics. Owners just will not take seriously an organisation full of grumbling, backbiting and contradictory messages.

So what we who work in libraries must treat as a watchword is that we are each other's customers within our own organisation. Even though this is fairly obvious when you think hard about it, it is not always that easy to put it into practice. This is partly because we are working to provide a variety of services, and with organisational structures which of course cannot take account of our individual characters. There still remains a lot to do in this area. It is almost certainly not the local authority politicians nor the university board who determined the detailed format of our organisations. Even though we tend to go through organisational changes all the time, sometimes driven by external factors, it is important to realise that we can often influence the shape of the revised structure to some extent. One thing we can be sure of is that it is quite clear to outsiders when we are not happy with our internal routines. It is just like how you feel if you are wearing shoes that are the wrong size or uncomfortable in some other way. Our general behaviour gives us away immediately, even if nobody realises that it is the shoes which are causing the problem. For us to feel good about our library work, and to operate together as a truly professional organisation, we must all recognise that we are each other's customers.

If we are to give proper consideration to others as individuals working alongside us, we must become less self-centred and remember all the time where our own and our colleagues' work fits into the organisational structure; we have to recognise that the whole is more important than just the sum of the parts. By all means everyone can come up with their own suggestions for changes in structure (and especially for cutting out unnecessary activities), but as we are in the end totally dependent on each other everything must be coordinated. Often we do not think enough about what our colleagues on the other side of the corridor are doing, and above all how important their jobs are in relation to everything else in the institution. It is of course easier to overcome this problem in smaller workplaces where you have plenty of opportunities to see each other's work close up – or even to share it. It is much more difficult in larger, more specialised working environments; here it is very important to have simple, open communication routes like blogs, intranets, e-mail contacts and so on, so that we can easily relate to each other and to our management.

But it is not enough just to create these means of communicating with each other: we must make sure they are being used in a meaningful way. In the stressful world we live in we can't always depend on having enough time to be able to discuss everything with everybody. This problem can at least to some extent be overcome by using relatively new techniques like e-mails, intranets, video conferences and others.

Consider that even the smallest change can snowball into something large in the end. Remember the famous science-fiction story about a time-traveller who goes back in time and breaks off a tiny twig, and then returns to a completely changed future. So think in terms of communication rather than merely information!

## User marketing

When I talk about user marketing, I mean marketing to our users: students, scientists, researchers and the other users of our library. Again, I think the library world is generally very good at user marketing; our problem is that often we don't think we are all that good at providing our services, for one reason or another! How can our customers possibly recognise our talent if we are not aware of it ourselves?

We must *tell* them! And tell them again and again! This group of people can help us enormously if they think our service is good, or better still believe it is excellent, and if *we* can communicate their judgement to our owners. This would complete the full circle of successful owner marketing.

Our users constitute the primary element of our 'part-time marketing team'. But other things being equal it doesn't just work out nicely that they will carry out this vital function for us, or at least not as much as we want, nor will they necessarily interact positively with the people we so urgently want to get through to.

We have to *ask* them to help us. Like everyone else in this circle they are very busy, and they have no time to give much thought to how good our services are – and how dependent we all are on their opinion in these days of budget cuts.

So let's ask them. Let's use any quotations we can extract from them about the library. Let's use all the nice stories we hear about how important the library is, and how significant our contribution to the whole institution. Our satisfied customers can help us with both owner and user marketing, but the first step is up to us. Traditionally in our library community we have never needed to ask for outside help – at least not as much as we do now. So there are no precedents.

Meanwhile we must not forget the other side of the coin. It is vital to keep an eye on any less satisfied users. We can often learn more from these people, in terms of finding the right products and services, than we can from all our kind friends who are generally satisfied and happy with what we provide. It is not as pleasant communicating with our critics, but on the other hand it is invaluable for our development.

Furthermore, there is no guarantee that our owners are interested in the same information as our users (they should be, but after analysing what owners want you will probably discover that it differs a lot from the 'standard' needs and interests).

Man is a complicated being and has no entirely simple way of learning things. That is why sometimes it can take time to become educated in a new subject. We librarians come mostly from a background in the humanities, and are deeply ingrained by culture and literature. The humanities-based view of life can be very positive, enriching and strengthening, but it can also paradoxically work against us because our world is influenced so much by literature. Within literature there are many examples of how people manage their feelings, demonstrating the various extreme states like love, hate, war and peace. The problem arises when we have to operate in a different environment, with the general public and some of our other stakeholders – the ones who don't read the same books as we do, or who maybe have a totally different frame of reference. We love looking after the needs of the borrowers who are similar to us, or at least those who act the way we expect them to act. But what about the others – the ones who are 'difficult'? The ones who demand something beyond what we can provide? Maybe it's even our bosses when they are questioning an activity that they don't know enough about. It is important to recognise and understand these groups and their views, but it's probably not worth being overly concerned with them. You risk getting upset on a long-term basis, and as a result becoming sidetracked and generally ineffective. Things that for one reason or another we cannot change we should leave alone, and instead try to find other solutions. These solutions may well lead to us getting a refreshed perspective on the whole issue, and so building more knowledge about things of which we were not previously aware. Maybe it is not that easy, but it is out of crises and problems that we develop as human beings, and as marketers. We simply have to adjust ourselves and become even better, and more service-oriented.

The good news is that for both user and owner marketing we can use the same tools.

Let us have another look at the marketing literature and theories we studied earlier. I would like to start with a quotation from Philip Kotler (2006), the well-known marketing guru whose books are in the marketing courses' literature lists all around the world. He says: 'Marketing is more a philosophy than a science.'

If you check the lists of specific activities you will see that your library is probably already at least attempting many of them. With luck you will come across something that you have not tried recently. Or if you have, why not try it again?

User marketing is of course all about 'listening to our customers' needs'. This sounds superficially very easy and very understandable, but it is in practice the hardest thing to do for all of us. Sometimes we have no time, sometimes we think we know better (which we do, of course, but not always and without exception).

Our internal and external environments are changing all the time. Threats become opportunities, weaknesses became strengths, or the other way around (Google could be a threat or an opportunity). So we need to have routines for marketing and for assessing the whole process on a regular basis. Remember while doing the regular analysis that you must be almost brutally honest with yourself and your institution: do not analyse your library as you would like to have it or how it should be, *but how it is now – the reality*.

# Some suggestions for marketing actions

Besides the usual library activities such as courses, authors' visits and other well-known events, I note below some alternative things which I have seen work well.

This list is not complete, but with luck you will find something here which you haven't tried before and which may suit your special circumstances. Also, I have deliberately included marketing activities for all kinds of libraries, as we can very well learn from and be enriched by each other. We will all benefit from more cooperation between public, academic and corporate libraries, and this is especially true when it comes to marketing.

Of course we have to follow whatever rules our institution sets, but surprisingly often we are following unwritten rules which we merely think exist, and in this way our initiative is inhibited. In reality much more is 'allowed' than is 'forbidden', even in the library world. Remember also that sometimes even notionally 'forbidden' activities may in fact be allowed, perhaps because of changes within your administrative structures, or because there are deemed to be special circumstances.

## New services

New services, such as the examples below, should be emerging all the time, and we must do more to draw our customers' attention to them.

- 'Book a librarian' – we will not normally be seen that much, and we have many customers who do not actually come into the library, and this could be a way of getting to meet some of them and offer our services and products.

- Let customers borrow mp3 players with audio books, or watch for similar new technical possibilities.

- Coordinate education, courses and training. There are libraries which have managed to establish themselves as independent educational institutions.

- In Sweden people can cast their votes in elections at their public library; check for other opportunities to provide similar services in your particular situation.

## Marketing librarians

An interesting concept which has been raised is that we should market librarians rather than just the library and its physical resources. After all, it is the library staff who make the difference.

At UKSG 2007 (the 30th United Kingdom Serial Group Annual Conference and Exhibition) T. Scott Plutchak of the University of Alabama at Birmingham said:

> How we think about our future is revealed in how we talk about it – when we're talking sloppily, it's because we're thinking sloppily. For example, we talk as if 'library' were a synonym for 'librarian', when in fact we should separate the two (to allow librarians' roles to evolve and change outside the restrictive concept of the traditional library). Whilst the library is a means by which librarians have connected users to information, it is one of many tools which can be deployed to this end. (Plutchak, 2007)

Scott referenced the 'Library 2.0' phenomenon, and noted that although he was not a fan of the label, the concepts it represents are useful to librarians. However, while it's great that librarians are utilising Web 2.0 technologies to connect with their users, 'Second Life is not a replacement for first life'. Personal relationships with library users are no less critical in this new age – so if users don't come to the library any more (because its services are so readily available digitally), librarians do need to seek out other means of engagement (see www.uksg.org/liveserials.blogspot.com).

## Find new customers

I am again quoting T. Scott Plutchak (2007):

> The important work that the librarian does actually happens when he *leaves* the library and engages with the world outside. The library is important but what is essential for the librarian to do his job is to leave the library.

## Generate services

Generate services for new groups within the university, local area or company, especially for people who don't normally come to the library. When we go out (even mentally), we will find potential users who simply do not think that a library is for them. Go out and convince them. The important thing is to start to think 'outside the library'.

## Joint marketing

Market jointly with other agents within your institution. Find another university body which needs marketing (in fact everybody needs it), or a partner within a local area or company. Then we can make an alliance and help each other; the costs will be halved, which is important as marketing is as we know costly both in money terms and indirectly in staff time.

## Cooperation

Try to find some form of cooperation with people outside the library (see Plutchak, 2007). Cooperation between library types is another option – in Sweden we are encouraged by the government to cooperate on the basis of 'all libraries within a geographical region'. We have discovered that once we start thinking outside the context of our own particular library, we can find many fields of cooperation.

## Get involved

Some libraries are very proactive and try to ensure that they are involved in any presentations to official visitors to their institution.

## Statistics

For our professional purposes we rely a lot on usage statistics, which are very good as far as they go, but we do not seem to use them very much in our marketing. They can be a fantastic tool, but to use them in this way we probably need to change how we look at them, and take a broader view. How would our owners look at them? Try to see things from their perspective. They are almost certainly interested in different aspects of usage statistics from the ones we see as essential.

In addition, all the yearly reports we produce could be used in both our owner marketing and our user marketing. When asked what they do with these reports every year, some librarians answered: 'Well, we leave it with the university president's secretary.' Outsiders unfortunately just aren't automatically interested in the library world, but we can stimulate their interest. Our products and services are extremely good and widely used, and often indispensable. There are innumerable ways to conduct our marketing: we just need to bring these methods together, and of course to make sure our saws are sharp before we begin.

## Take advantage of new media and technology

At the Second Nordic Conference on Scholarly Communication in Lund, Sweden, in 2004, a significant question was asked: 'Is there a magic button somewhere for us just to push and market our e-resources?'

As librarians we have access to so much information, and have secured so many 'Big Deals' and other comprehensive agreements with publishers, that our challenge is to reach all our users to tell them what is available. Our aim is to reach everyone in our institution or region to show them how many e-resources we have and how easy it is to access them through the library. The question asked at the conference may not have been serious, but we do appear in some respects to be still looking for that magic button.

We still need to do the 'leg work', but there is one thing working in our favour: e-resources are in vogue and popular with our users. There are many marketing initiatives already established in libraries, but we need to do more.

Word of mouth and personal recommendations are invaluable. There is no doubt that personal contact is extremely important and effective, but it is not possible to use that channel alone – we must adopt other methods.

- *Targeted e-mail alerts* sent to academics or other groups by our information specialists. This is ideal in theory, but unfortunately due to lack of time this technique usually tends to become subsumed into the library's e-newsletter and lost. The problem is that our customers are overwhelmed by information and would like to have data tailored to their special interests. It is well worth our while to find the resources to make this effort, if necessary by dropping less productive activities.

- *E-mails to new staff* giving useful links and introducing other services.

- *Training courses*. All libraries are using this marketing method. It is very important that these courses are presented by people with good communication skills.

- *Events associated with specific subject areas*. Many libraries use all kinds of events within the institution or public library district to market themselves and their services. The important thing is to have a good overview of what other events are going on within the organisation.

- *The institution's website.* Procedures for regular checking and updating are very important, otherwise webpages could have a negative impact. A section on 'new resources' is popular with many libraries.

- *The intranet.* Intranets are most common in government and local library cooperatives and consortia; used in the right way this can be a very efficient way of communicating.

- *The library's own OPAC* (Online Public Access Catalog).

- *Electronic monitors and plasma screens* in the library publicity displays.

## Furniture as a marketing tool

A library is a wonderful meeting place, and a pleasant environment where people can study, read, talk, listen, relax and borrow books. It is a place which should reflect lifelong learning and respect for knowledge, and furthermore a place with professional staff who provide a professional service.

Furniture and fittings are of course very important for both library workers and visitors. We should have the kind of equipment, with the mix of colours and lights, which will attract, intrigue and welcome all our visitors.

There have been many changes in the library world. Demands are changing; the media range has changed. The library is no longer just a place full of books and journals: we have taken on many new functions, and libraries are becoming much more of a meeting place as well as a library in its original form.

The basis for the perfectly functional library, from the point of view of both library personnel and visitors alike, is the clear organisation of the content of the whole library in a physical environment which is at the same time both visually attractive and comfortable.

Sometimes, in our eagerness to display and make available as much material as possible, we go for high shelves, which tend to make the room feel claustrophobic. The whole atmosphere will be much more open and free with lower shelves. We can display books on some shelves with just spines showing and on others with full face.

Walls, floors, ceilings, windows, paintings, curtains and carpets should match the furniture and fittings harmoniously and create a pleasant atmosphere. Not only the colours but also the materials must match.

Ideally you should plan the overall look of the library, even if you cannot achieve everything all in one go. Colours are very important, especially now that we have so many machines in our libraries. Don't be afraid of colours. Imagine a pink and purple library – it is possible.

In order to mitigate and soften the technical environment you can have one piece of 'old' furniture – maybe a big old-fashioned armchair (you can buy an old one and have it professionally recovered). The library should have lots of light, with the right temperature, and it must also have spare space for future new technical equipment. It is important to have a flexible lighting system. Never put shelves in front of a window! This is so obvious, but all too often, when we need new shelves or space for something else, we are still committing this fundamental crime. I have seen it many times.

A library should be a place for interplay between people, but also a place that can provide privacy, which is just as important. This factor must be properly included in the overall planning and the calculation of costs. It is important to view the library as a meeting place, and the provision of a coffee shop matches this concept perfectly.

Look at the successful American bookshop chain of Barnes & Noble; their idea is to copy the combination of a library and a coffee shop, because it makes people feel good about themselves, it offers a relaxed environment and it has all the desirable connotations of knowledge and learning.

The easy availability of materials is an essential element in library marketing. A really good display of all the products and services on offer should make it easy to find all the different departments. Displays must be clear and graphically good, with good colours and attractive design, and placed in the right locations with excellent lighting. Digital information on orientation can combine successfully with printed guides. If these aids are put together they will help visitors find their way around the library easily, and thus contribute to the feeling of comfortable fulfilment at which we are aiming.

## Media and publishing

It is a good rule to start to think about how you are going to try to use the *press* from the very beginning of your planning of any new activities. Even the press needs new ideas and inspiration, and we can certainly provide them. According to Erik Lindfelt, director of Jönköping City Library in Sweden, who is also a journalist and has written in depth about the media, there are certain suggestions which we should always bear in mind.

- We have different roles: journalists are definitely *not* our enemies.

- Take the initiative – it is always better to be first than to be asked.

- Build a network of contacts in the media world.

- Be very clear about what you want to say, and what is your essential message. Choose only the *most* important items: don't try to say everything.

- Be clear and simple, and avoid library jargon.

- Be available for follow-up if you give out a press release.

- There are bound to be occasional mistakes, but nobody is really going to worry about them.

- Try to see a draft of the article, and don't be afraid to ask for corrections if they are needed.

- Journalists are also human beings, and they are inclined to generalise.

- Check (in a nice way, of course) to make sure the key facts have been understood.

- Have a precise understanding of the media deadlines and the consequent time pressure, but don't be afraid to ask for more time if you need it.

- If something goes wrong be open and honest, admit obvious mistakes and concede that you do not know everything.

Often it is best not merely to generate a press release but to write the actual article yourself and send it to journalists. They are also short of time and are sometimes very happy to receive such help.

## Collect everything interesting and positive

Every single thing that is ever written about the library is important, and can be used in both user and owner marketing. You can write articles yourself, or make a journalist pay attention to some of your activities.

### *Brochures*

It is very important that our printed marketing material is produced professionally. There is still sometimes in the library world the belief that we should do it ourselves, because it is cheaper and because that is what we always did. Use professionals: the difference is enormous. Believe me, it is worth it.

### *Publishing*

Publish your own newsletter or journal, or contribute frequently to those of your institution.

### *Paper*

Do not underestimate *paper* in all aspects of marketing. So many people who constantly use e-resources in their routine activities will admit (maybe only privately or even just to themselves) that they do read paper but *do not always* read information that comes electronically. One example is 'old-fashioned' bookmarks in paper, which work very well and customers come and 'ask' for these. Professionally produced printed brochures and similar items also work very well.

## Activities and events

I am also suggesting some organised events – these are mainly from the public library arena, but again I think they can be modified and used, or at least can serve as an inspiration, even for university and corporate libraries.

## Competitions

We can have competitions in a large variety of subjects – I imagine you may already have done this sort of thing on many occasions, but do try them again even if you think you are doing the same thing all the time. If these competitions are on different subjects the library will still be seen as very creative. According to many libraries it is easy to obtain prizes for quizzes from local shops, which can see that this is an opportunity for their marketing.

## Courses

These are like competitions: you can arrange courses with different contents and market your library this way. I am sure you probably already do a lot in this area, but you could maybe add some subjects which are interesting to rather different customers from our usual audience. A course helps to market the library as an active member of the university, local authority or company, and it may also stimulate course delegates to market the library to their colleagues and friends (as they become our part-time marketers).

## Conferences

Conferences can also make very successful contributions to both our owner and our user marketing. There is a great PR value just in announcing a conference, even if it can be difficult sometimes to attract the ideal size of audience – again we are all competing for our customers' time and attention. Remember that it can take time to learn how to initiate a conference and then how to market it successfully.

But if we don't try, we will never know. Conferences can sometimes be repeated, and if that is the case it will be progressively less demanding for the staff.

## Exhibitions

We often stage exhibitions in our libraries, but we can also do our own exhibitions.

Show literally, as an exhibition, what the library would look like without any library staff at all. There will be disorganised heaps of books and journals, and nobody could actually obtain any useful information.

## Book festivals

Various kinds of book festivals can involve the library; these are an opportunity to invite authors and hold interesting associated activities.

## Marathon reading

Children stay in the library right through the night reading stories. This is an activity which has been tried successfully and without mishap in several different countries in Europe.

## The longest book table

A 1,020 metres long table full of books can be seen in Stockholm each year in September. This event got into the *Guinness Book of Records*, and of course generates a lot of attention in the media.

## *Stranger than fiction?*

A public library in southern Sweden announced a special event: 'Borrow a prejudice and get rid of it.' There were people representing different occupations and religions, and visitors could borrow a person for 15 minutes to talk to them and see if they still kept up their prejudice, or if they changed their minds as a result of this first-hand contact and information. This event got a lot of publicity, and many libraries benefited from it; there were 30 press representatives from all over Europe and even from Australia.

## *User sessions*

Try marketing through specific user sessions organised by the library.

## *Open house*

Show what you are doing at the library behind the scenes through library workshops.

## *Library ball*

One library saw the opportunity for owner marketing at a library ball! It went very well and the library got many new users.

## *Be creative*

Now you are thinking, yes, I have heard about all these activities, but what about something completely new, totally different?

I do not know what your library looks like nor what sort of customers you have, so I propose an extremely creative exercise.

Imagine that you have obtained all the money for marketing you could possibly need, and concentrate only on the different marketing activities you would like to do. Do not exclude anything because it seems impossible or because the money is not available. Just try this exercise together with some colleagues. You will be surprised at how creative you can be and what fun it is. Most of all, believe me or not, most of the crazy/funny/impossible activities you are suggesting *are possible with some adjustments*.

## New technology trends are here to help us in marketing

This section borrows heavily from the website of Gabe Rios (medlibtechtrends.wordpress.com/). According to Rios, there are ten top technology trends with which librarians should be conversant.

- *Social software.* As overall user traffic continues to decrease in our physical libraries, the need to explore new 'virtual' methods of user engagement increases. Social software has the potential to provide a much-needed link between the library and its virtual users. This is not to say that libraries should rush out to buy new software and implement new services: you should be selective about what software you choose to implement and should always solicit feedback from your users about these services. Blogs, wikis and Facebook are three examples of social software with the potential to engage users where they are.

- *Open source software*. This freely available software gives you the ability to alter the source code and customise the software or add functionality. Open source is not new by any means, but there is a lot of untapped potential in this area. There are working examples of open source integrated library systems such as Koha and Evergreen, and learning/content management systems such as Moodle and Sakai. Using open source software, libraries have the potential to benefit from a larger development community dealing with similar users and issues.

- *Mobile information devices*. The role of mobile devices in libraries will continue to grow as device functionality increases. We live in a mobile world, and people want to access resources and work while they are on the go. Devices such as the iPhone and Sony's new microcomputer (Vaio UX) will offer new possibilities and venues for mobile information access.

- *Collaboration tools*. In addition to engaging virtual users, as mentioned above, we need to find new ways to collaborate with our users. Depending on your installation, Microsoft SharePoint has the potential to integrate many different collaboration and communication tools. There are also services such as Connotea and Zotero, which allow users to save, organise and share references. This type of software can offer another way for librarians to be involved with a research team.

- *Second Life*. This is an open-ended virtual world that offers social interactions between your avatar (virtual self) and other avatars. A group of librarians have already developed Info Island and a virtual reference desk. This is another example of technology that has the potential to meet people where they are.

- *Cloud architecture.* Cloud architecture consists of two parts: folksonomies and tag clouds. Folksonomies are user-generated labels for objects such as bookmarks and photos; tag clouds are a way to represent more popular labels (or tag clouds) visually to identify objects. Libraries always struggle to ensure that the terms we use to describe our services and collections are relevant to users and contain less jargon. Experimenting with cloud architecture could help users to find the services and resources they need.

- *Wireless.* Wireless technology continues to get faster and more ubiquitous. Working in synergy with mobile information devices, wireless technology has the potential to take clinical decision-making to the point of care. Many people have experienced working with mobile devices that were not wirelessly connected to the internet: these devices are only as good as the last time they were connected to a network. Wireless ubiquity will allow users to interact with the resources they need when they need them.

- *Mashups.* Mashups allow you to create a new service from two or more existing services. Several Web 2.0 services feature lightweight programming models that allow users to combine and remix them into new and different services. Libraries can investigate with remixing to offer new services to users.

- *Streaming media.* Streaming media continues to gain popularity as services such as YouTube and podcasting develop. The effects of streaming media on libraries are unclear, but there is potential to use this technology for virtual instruction. We could also facilitate the development and organisation of streaming media repositories for other areas of our institutions.

- *Catalogue overlays.* Products such as Endeca and AquaBrowser are springing up to put a new face on library catalogues and resources. Many libraries are now questioning whether the traditional library catalogue can continue to link to everything in the library's collection.

# Some more thoughts on marketing

## Marketing is fun

Marketing is fun, and gives us power to change our situation.

Involve vendors and let them help us in our marketing. Some libraries are encouraging vendors' workshops and see this as a way of marketing the library.

## Marketing is developing

Competition is good for development, and it is good for us too. Sometimes we mention Google and Yahoo! as competitors. I would prefer to call them complementary. We in the libraries are the ones who can teach people about the reliability of information and why it is so important, especially now. Is 90 per cent of information from Google rubbish, as some would say? It is dangerous to condemn all other sources of information, especially if the whole world around us is using them. Much publisher content is searchable through Google and Google Scholar and many other developments are ongoing right now, such as the link between Windows Live Academic and Blackwell Publishing.

Because of the competition we face from all other information sources it is difficult to get academics to come to presentations and read all our information, but we should never stop trying.

## Marketing takes time

Marketing takes time, and you cannot expect results overnight.

Keep on repeating the marketing message, even if it doesn't seem to be working – and the point at which we are bored with the message we are communicating is often the one when both our owners and our users finally start to listen to us.

## Marketing means more visibility

People are used to searching and using the university website and, of course, Google and other search engines. We need to be visible, now more than ever. There are many scientists who do not recognise the importance of a library, as they think that everything is easily accessible through Google. At the 2006 UKSG annual conference, Carol Goble gave a heretical speech along the following lines.

Life scientists read journals.

I'm a computer scientist. I don't.

It's on the web.

It's in podcast talks or PowerPoint.

Google is the Lord's work.

PhD students are for doing library work; researchers don't need to go there.

Journal publications are too outdated.

Her conclusion was that everything is available on the web, that Lord Google can deal with any help that is needed, and that PhD students could be used for picking up any less important reports from the library. That was a shock for us, and I think we need to take to heart the opinion of a serious scientist, as she just didn't realise how much work the library was carrying out on her behalf to enable her to access everything from her desk without ever going to the library herself. I am sure this was mostly meant to be provocative, but there are probably many more scientists like Carol and for that reason we must be more *visible*!

## *The importance of being personal*

We must never forget to be visible in spite of the electronic world which surrounds us. Nowadays, when everyone can just sit at home and get most of the information they want through one search engine or another, we absolutely must meet our customers somehow, somewhere. We need more of the 'human touch' in our digital world. We must constantly generate visits by important guests, and meetings and all the other usual activities, in order to be noticed! Our users and decision-makers have to be made to recognise what we are doing, and exactly what proportion of their success depends on us.

# 5

# Who else can help us? Publishers' marketing suggestions

Many libraries are now sensibly looking for closer cooperation with vendors and providers, and I have asked some of them to give us their advice on how to market ourselves better. Remember that it is in their interest for us to be successful. We have received many useful suggestions, and we can acknowledge that vendors really want to help, and that they understand our problems both with the availability of time and resources and with staying abreast of the new, fast-developing technologies.

## Elsevier

### *Daria DeCooman, senior library communications manager, San Diego, USA*

The marketing resources publishers offer librarians are extensive, practical and free.

Today's librarians looking for marketing assistance should keep publishers in mind. Whether we're talking about promoting a particular book or e-resource, or promoting library services in general, marketing tips and tricks as well as concepts and strategy are freely available on publisher websites or from the minds of publishing colleagues who'd be glad to speak with you.

Why are publishers so eager to help librarians with marketing? Well, we all want to make the most of our investments and resources – publishers producing information products and librarians purchasing them. But there's something bigger at play too. Publishers, just like librarians, want to contribute to the continuous cycle of scholarly discovery, scientific, technical and medical innovation and overall intellectual advancement.

How do we all do this? How do we contribute to the greater good, to an improved future for our world? We – librarians and publishers alike – encourage learners of all ages by providing them with the most up-to-date information resources. We help connect researchers with information tools that meet their needs best. And as we face an ever-expanding universe of information, we collaborate to get the word out to users that, thanks to their libraries, reputable and reliable information resources are readily available.

What can librarians find when they turn to publishers for marketing help? Publishers offer a range of types of assistance, from cover shots or reviews of publications to expert consultations on how to produce outreach campaigns and assistance with special events.

Here are examples of marketing help freely available from publishers today.

- Assistance with writing promotional messages to go to library users via e-mail, webpages or RSS.

- Assistance with designing targeted campaigns to reach specific populations of users, such as faculty or undergraduates.

- Assistance with analysing usage statistics and advice on how results can guide development of marketing efforts.

- Guidelines on how to promote effective use of online resources.

- Guidelines on how to design library websites to maximise usability.

- Support for 'fresher fairs' held on site on campuses or in libraries.

- Toolkits offering templates for press releases, posters and ads to appear in print newsletters and banners to appear on websites.

How do librarians and publishing staff turn marketing tips and tricks, concepts and strategy into action? Librarians collaborating with publisher staff on marketing efforts probably notice a focus on staying practical and making sure there are demonstrable impacts. As you get to know publisher-provided marketing resources and the publisher staff (often possessing LIS degrees or library experience) involved in creating these resources, you'll hear repeatedly that librarians and publishers need to keep marketing efforts doable, affordable and trackable to whatever extent is feasible.

Keeping it real also means we must acknowledge that no publisher can afford to provide in-depth marketing support to each and every library customer all the time. That said, if you need marketing help please remember to consider giving a publisher a call or visiting a publisher website. We're all in this together.

# MetaPress

## *Heather Klusendorf*

The goal for electronic libraries and the golden bough to reach for as librarians is working to offer patrons the best possible options for locating full text. In the electronic library world, the shelf no longer comes into play and the physical movement from card catalogue to aisle to print journal is replaced by search and link-to technology. The ease of the electronic library is intended to replace the long hours of physical labour often involved in research by making the process of locating the needed resources a seamless one that involves just a little bit of arm-to-wrist-to-finger action. What many libraries may not realise is that with this new world of internet ease also comes a new chore for many librarians. While computer screens, authentication and databases have made the experience of the electronic library easier for the busy researcher, this same electronic highway opens up new territory that the extremely busy librarian must travel. In an electronic library world that is driven by usage (for we all know that usage is god), the goal often becomes one of generating larger statistical numbers to prove the new-found worth of the electronic library. If the success of the electronic library means generating usage, then libraries must take the time to 'get the word out' about resources and ensure that a researcher's imagined effortless electronic process actually does work in a way that rewards users with the needed resources – whether they be the actual full text, a link to pay-per-view full text, the library catalogue and shelf, or inter-library loan options.

A big step towards helping to realise this goal is for libraries to use owner marketing to help meet the growing needs of the electronic library community. The electronic library must provide fluid movement to resources without any dead ends. One way to help is to make users aware of the availability of content by providing them with the next step in locating full text. Librarians can help fight research stagnation, which is the unnecessary end of valiant searching, by taking advantage of link resolvers like

EBSCO's LinkSource or Ex Libris's SFX. However, there are free tools offered for MetaPress administrators that do not require a library to purchase a linking resolver. Setting up a helpful link for users to contact the library administrator or the inter-library loan desk is free and does not require a link resolver at the library's end.

Libraries may be unaware of free tools offered by online electronic hosts like MetaPress that afford a simple and easy way to take users to the next step in their research. Linkout tools on MetaPress allow libraries to take users to that next step. Helping users to take this step by providing more linking options can increase library usage and build user loyalty for a library's electronic resources that may be fighting outside search engines like Google or Dogpile. One benefit of linkout technology is that libraries can choose where the next step is for their users. Instead of going to Google, libraries can offer a helpful link to Google Scholar, where academic research is available that may steer a user back to the library databases.

Ideally, the goal is to keep users within the library environment. Librarians take a lot of care to offer peer-reviewed academic research for their patrons, and a lot of this content may be available within the physical library in print resources or at a sister library within the university network. Libraries can take advantage of linkout resources that will help them build a bridge between the electronic and the print. The MetaPress admin site linkout page (http://admin.metapress.com) provides the materials to help build that bridge.

The MetaPress admin site provides simple tools that can be used quickly to set up linking from any MetaPress website. In order to be able to provide these tools, MetaPress is considered an OpenURL linking source. For an online content host to be considered fully OpenURL compliant, it must be considered both a linking target and a linking source. Most libraries are familiar with aggregators and publisher sites offering linking targets, which means that content can be linked to in standard OpenURL format. Even though this sounds complicated, the MetaPress admin site makes setting up and working with linkout linking extremely easy by providing a handy URL builder which provides OpenURL journal and article metadata placeholders that can be selected from publication, issue and article boxes to create the linkout URL needed.

# OCLC

## *Marketing libraries – advice from the OCLC*

Libraries offer a valuable communal space for learning, working and entertainment. They help people to make connections, sometimes at critical points in their lives – before an exam, during a job search, when teaching a child to read. We view libraries as a constant and trusted source of information and support. Libraries are a sound product, but the challenge in marketing terms is to keep them current and relevant in a changing world. One of the biggest perceived threats to the relevance of libraries is the web.

There has been much talk about how libraries are not visible enough on the open web, and how much more they need to do to bring their services to users at the point of need – which frequently means when they are sitting at home at their desktops, facing perhaps the same critical points in their lives but unaware of how the library can help them.

One of the most important developments in recent years has been the rise of virtual reference services. We shouldn't underestimate how impressed end-users are when they can access the real answers to their questions while sitting at home. Search engines have set an expectation that answers can be found at any time of the day or night – at least when you look hard enough. Virtual reference services have taken that one step further by actually responding directly to the user, and also by offering an out-of-hours service.

In the UK the Museums, Libraries and Archives Council has been running a virtual reference service, Enquire, for years, using the OCLC's QuestionPoint platform. Feedback from users has been very enthusiastic. One grateful recipient said:

> ...this was most helpful, and I was able to make good use of it for my sermon this morning! I had not made the connection between Sabbath celebration and the exodus from Egypt.
>
> I read part of your e-mail in my sermon this morning, explaining where I had received this information from, so I publicised and applauded your service from the pulpit!

This is just one of many comments Enquire receives from the public, who seem genuinely surprised that libraries are transferring what were purely communal services to a web environment. When we talk about 'delighting our customers' this is surely an example of what libraries can achieve when they find themselves delivering to a previously unaware web audience, who may have no expectation that their neighbourhood library holds much in store for them.

The success of these and other similar web-based services is reliant on the cooperation of libraries. The magnitude of the web environment means that the true impact is best achieved in collaboration with other like-minded libraries. Enquire is a good exemplar of that approach, but there are countless others that the OCLC and similar organisations are increasingly predicating. Contributing to the 'global presence' of libraries in a global web environment is a marketing effort in which any library can participate, no matter how large or small.

# Taylor & Francis Journals

## *Jennifer McMillan, library marketing manager*

The role of a librarian has changed radically in the last 15 years, and journal librarians now work in multifaceted roles where resources and energies can seem like they are pulled in every direction. After spending time deciding on purchases, cataloguing resources, navigating through myriad publishers' terms and conditions, sorting out your link resolver and federated searches... adding the title 'marketer' to your job description can seem enough to make you reach for a coffee! However, taking some time to ensure library users understand the resources on offer to them is time well spent, and could make your daily role less difficult once they have a greater understanding of your products. The following are some tips to help you approach marketing your resources, but the best thing to remember is to keep things simple so that your precious time is not stretched even further.

- *Work out what you want to say.* Be clear you understand what you are trying to achieve before you put together any marketing campaign. Spending half an hour putting together a plan will really help you to construct your campaigns as efficiently as possible. The next section gives an example marketing plan which might help you to begin to put together some ideas.

- *Enlist some help.* Tying your own promotions to the work being carried out by faculty members and coordinating on timing will result in more successful campaigns, and you will benefit from support from colleagues with whom you can share ideas and work.

- *Remember your audience.* Every university library will have various different audiences, each with its own needs. Consider when you are putting together a campaign how you might need to vary your message between first-year undergraduates and a professor with an impressive tenure.

- *Remember your audience is human!* Even if the resources you are trying to promote are very scholarly, you can still create appealing marketing campaigns. The best campaigns engage people's needs and emotions, so try to consider what necessitated the purchase of a particular resource in the first place, and convey this in your campaign.

- *Tell, tell, tell.* Marketers strive to measure the efficacy of their campaigns, and one of the key pointers to the success or failure of a campaign is audience recall. Getting your library users to remember what you are telling them is greatly helped by telling them more than once. So send e-mails, put up posters, add a message to your library homepage, leave leaflets for people to pick up…

- *Make use of any research you undertake.* Research into user behaviour can include analysing usage statistics, observing how people use the library and giving library users a chance to air their views via surveys, comment boxes and focus groups. Whatever research methods you use, do make sure you make the most of any feedback you receive. Spending some time mulling over the results can illustrate knowledge gaps or changing user behaviour, and you will be much better equipped to deal with changes if you are armed with this information.

- *Make the most of internal resources.* Many universities now have business and marketing courses for undergraduates. Why not involve students from these courses in a project to help promote your library? They could help with marketing plans, promotional materials, PR and leaflet distribution. You could also recruit their help to become library advocates, offering recommendations about resources and services to their peers, who may be more willing to listen to what they have to say than to direct communications from the library.

- *Pester the publishers.* All publishers have marketing experts. They were the people who convinced you to buy the resource you want to promote, so get their help in making the most of it! Ask them for posters, leaflets and user guides, and if you are not happy with the resources on offer then let them know.

## Example marketing plan

*Background*: Library X wants to embark on a project to encourage undergraduates to make the most of the online journal collections available to them. Research has shown that the undergraduate community do not fully understand the benefits of using journals, and how they can enrich their work.

*Objective*: To increase journal usage by 20 per cent within the economics undergraduate community during the course of the next three months.

*Aims*: The aims of this campaign will include:

- increasing understanding of the value of peer-reviewed research, and the difference between it and other online sources of information;

- providing undergraduates with the tools and knowledge to search and access the journals available to them via the library portal;

- encouraging undergraduates to use peer-reviewed research in their own essays in an effective way, taking into account issues of plagiarism.

*Method*: The Library Department will work with the Economics Faculty to encourage undergraduates to make more use of the electronic journals available to them in the library. This campaign will include the following elements.

- Training for economics undergraduates on the library catalogue, focusing on the search features available to them. This will involve face-to-face training sessions as well as interactive demonstrations via the library portal.

- Posters, postcards and leaflets will be sourced from various publishers to help the library promote the economics collection. Posters will be displayed in the library and leaflets and postcards will be available for students to browse.

- The library will target economics students with an e-mail campaign, encouraging them to make use of resources available to them.

- Faculty staff will integrate journal articles into students' reading lists. They will also work with library staff on a programme to train students on how to cite properly, producing an electronic guide to which students can refer when writing their essays and introducing them to online tools to help them check the format of their references.

*Results*: The success of the campaign will be determined by analysis of usage statistics for economics journals. Feedback will be gathered from faculty in terms of their perceptions of any changes seen in undergraduates' work. Questionnaires will also be circulated to undergraduates to assess their views on the contribution journals can make to their studies.

*Follow-up*: If this campaign is successful, it will provide the library with a template for future campaigns to target other groups in the undergraduate community. Marketing is not that difficult, as long as you spend some time making a plan and then following it through. Doing some work to promote the resources you have spent time and effort acquiring will help you to demonstrate your library's worth and allow your users to benefit fully from the materials on offer.

# 6

# Conclusion

Marketing for libraries is needed now more than ever, and although it may be a rather foreign concept for some of us it is not difficult or unpleasant work. It really can be interesting and even fun, and most of all it is an activity which helps both our development as individuals and the development of all the rest of our work.

The process of marketing forces us to think hard about our environment, to listen to our customers, both owners and users, and to interpret new signals for new needs in our community. It gives us an insight into our national and international world because we must watch what other people are doing and how they are doing it. Marketing can also be deeply satisfying when we see that we really are able to influence our situation in ways we may not have realised before.

It is up to all of you who work in libraries to decide how ambitious you are going to be in your marketing activities, and which of the many forms of implementation feels most relevant to your library, your talents and the specific work you are doing. What is absolutely certain is that if we maintain the concept of marketing in our daily thoughts and routines, we will eventually reap the rewards in a better and more lively and effective library. The results will probably not come at once, but if you can keep focused and not give up at the first hurdle it *will* definitely work out in the long run, bringing even more satisfaction for all the involved personnel.

Good luck!

# References

Abrams, Rhonda (2007) 'Successful business research', Costco Wholesale UK brochure; available at: *www .PlanningShop.com* (accessed: 18 February 2008).

Ansoff, Igor (1957) 'The Ansoff matrix'; available at: *www .coursenotes.co.uk/ansoffsmatrix.php* (accessed: 18 February 2008).

Bedbury, Scott and Fenichell, Stephen (2002) *A New Brand World: Eight Principles for Achieving Brand Leadership in the 21st Century*. New York: Viking Penguin.

Boone, Louis E. and Kurtz, David L. (1998) *Contemporary Marketing Wired*, 9th edn. Fort Worth, TX: Dryden Press.

Boston Consulting Group (1970) 'BCG matrix'; available at: *www.bcg.com* (accessed: 18 February 2008).

Covey, S.R. (1989) *The Seven Habits of Highly Effective People: Restoring the Character Ethic*. London: Simon & Schuster.

Frazier, Kenneth (2001) 'The librarians' dilemma: contemplating the costs of the "Big Deal"', *D-Lib Magazine*, 7(3); available at: *www.dlib.org/* (accessed: 18 February 2008).

Goble, C. (2006) 'Science, workflows and collections', paper presented at 29th UKSG Annual Conference and Exhibition, University of Warwick, 3–5 April; available at: *www.uksg.org/events/previous.asp#2006conf* (accessed: 15 February 2008).

Gummesson, E. (2002) *Total Relationship Marketing: Marketing Strategy Marketing Management to the 30Rs – The Thirty Relationships – of a New Marketing Paradigm*, 2nd edn. Oxford: Butterworth-Heinemann.

Kotler, Philip (2006) Quoted on Kotler website; available at: *www.kotlermarketing.com/* (accessed: 12 August 2006).

Plutchak, T. Scott (2007) 'The librarian: fantastic adventures in the digital world', *Serials*, 20(2): 87.

Porter, Michael E. (1979) 'Five forces analysis'; available at: *www.marketingteacher.com* (accessed: 18 February 2008).

Tenopir, C. (2004) 'Is Google the competition?', *Library Journal*, 129(6): 30.

*The Charleston Report* (2007) 'Top 10 websites by brand', *The Charleston Report*, 12(2): 2.

# Further information

## Literature

Armstrong, Gary and Kotler, Philip (2002) *Marketing: An Introduction*, 6th edn. Upper Saddle River, NJ: Prentice-Hall.

Brynko, B. (2006) 'Blackwell opens the doors to Windows Live Academic', *Information Today*, 23(6): 43.

Grönroos, Christian (2007) *Service Management and Marketing: Customer Management in Service Competition*, 3rd edn. Chichester: Wiley Grönroos.

Helinsky, Z. (2004) 'On the circuit', *Serials*, 17(3): 299.

## Links

Joint Workshop on Electronic Publishing, organised by Delos, SVEP and ScieCom, Lund, 14–15 April 2005: *www.lub.lu.se/epubl_2005_Lund/*.

Kotler Marketing Group: *www.kotlermarketing.com/company.html*.

Marketing Teacher: *www.marketingteacher.com*.

Gabe Rios: *medlibtechtrends.wordpress.com/*.

Second Life: *http://secondlife.com/whatis/*.

Second Nordic Conference on Scholarly Communication: Towards a New Publishing Environment, Lund University, 26–28 April 2004: *www.lub.lu.se/ncsc2004/*.

UKSG Annual Conference and Exhibition: *www.uksg.org/events/annualconference.asp*.

# Index